BUEN
CAMINO

BUEN CAMINO
The French Way

GARY GREEN

Moix Publishing Company, LLC
1001 La Harpe Boulevard
Little Rock, Arkansas 72201
www.moixpublishing.com

First Edition: 2020
ISBN: 978-1-7337964-2-2

Book design: H. K. Stewart

Printed in the United States of America

This book is printed on archival-quality paper that meets requirements of the American National Standard for Information Sciences, Permanence of Paper, Printed Library Materials, ANSI Z39.48-1984.

For Patricia, Patou, Batou, My Sweet

love of my life

PREFACE

I'm going to tell you how this happened. I admit it could have happened on any trail in the world, but it didn't. It happened on El Camino Francés, the French Way to Santiago de Compostela, every day, just as I said it did.

A thought would come to my head, and we'd run with it.

It was lots of fun, and it gave me two hours at the bar and gave Batou two hours away from me.

Gary Green
July 11, 2019

The French Way

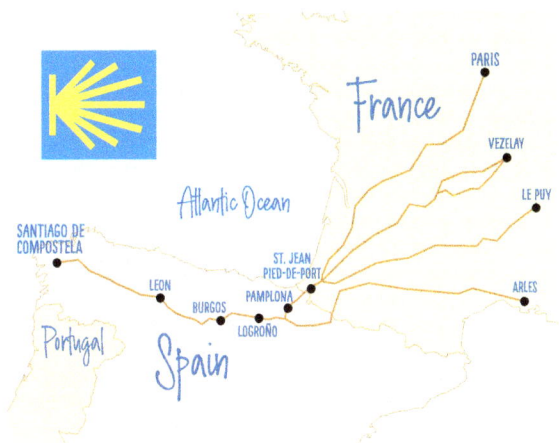

St. Jean Pied-de-Port
Roncesvalles
Zubiri
Pamplona
Puente de la Reina
Estella
Los Arcos
Logroño
Nájera
Santo Domingo de la
   Calzada
Belorado
Atapuerta
Burgos
Hornillos
Castrojeriz
Fromista
Carrion de los Condes
Calzadilla de la Cueza

La Cordoniz Sahagun
El Burgo Ranero
Mansilla de las Mulas
Leon
Mazarife/Villavante
Astorga
Rabanal del Camino
Ponferrada
Villafranca del Bierzo
Herrerias
O Cebreiro
Triacastela
Sarria
Portomarin
Palas de Rei
Arzua
Amenal
Santiago de Compostela

SAINT-JACQUES
DE
COMPOSTELLE

BRONZE
MASSIF

St. Jean Pied-de-Port
to Roncesvalles

Dear Rhys and Garrison,

It was a good day.

We took the Napoleon route from St. Jean Pied-de-Port to Roncesvalles. Supposedly 15.6 miles, but a fellow pilgrim said she measured it on her iPhone as 20.

We saw many cherry trees, wild flowers, sheep, cows, horses on hilltops, falcons, a shrine to a fallen pilgrim who tried this trek in winter and was buried by an avalanche, and snow on mountaintops. I'll send some photos so you can read this letter like a picture book.

At first, I thought the Pyrenees had nothing on the Rockies, but I soon came to respect them, even though we were only in the foothills. They will wear you out.

The trail was well marked. My poor Spanish was no problem.

Sun was bright and hot. We shared the few small shade trees with other hikers. Glad I had my hat and sunglasses. I'm already using the backup sunglasses because the good pair didn't make it through the security conveyor in Biarritz.

Despite sunscreen, I'm working on my farmer/hiker—and I'm proud to be both—suntan and toned muscles, which surely will develop over the next thirty-eight days.

Batou says I march to the beat of a different drummer. Or perhaps to the tinkle of slow, slow cowbells. Or the bells on the backpacks of pilgrims.

As we said goodbye to the last of the French Basque Country, Batou was pulling way out in front of me. Every time I'd stop to take a photo, she'd advanced about seventy-five yards. You look at all the pictures and do the math.

It wasn't long before her white shirt was a speck on the next mountain over. She looked like the white tail of a rabbit.

I saw two huge birds of prey hunting over the heather. Beautiful. I tried to take a photo, then remembered a video of an eagle swooping a man off a mountain. I thought of that bunny tail and decided to pick up my pace. I shortcut the switchbacks, pumping my walking sticks like ski poles. The birds flew off, but not before I got a tail feather for my hat.

Well, if the sign at the French border was correct, we've got about 500 miles to go.

I've got my clothes pulled out for tomorrow, but now I'm too tired to pull open the Velcro pockets on my quick-dry pants. I feel pain from my toes to my brain, but that's just from time to time.

Sunrise comes early. Soon it will be time to act like cow patties and hit the trail.

Thanks for staying with me this long. Grandchildren are great inspiration.

Love,
Ba

RONCESVALLES TO ZUBIRI

Dear Garrison and Rhys,

There were many ups and downs but nothing like yesterday, until the last few kilometers into Zubiri when the trail was quite rocky and steep. Not a trek I'd want to take in the rain, but rain wasn't a problem today. We had blue sky and heat. It was a more pleasant day as far as the sun because of beautiful old tree–lined lanes.

There were more villages and hamlets. Tiny gardens with matching tiny greenhouses, rock walls, lots of birds, well-maintained rock pavers on the trail, stone slab bridges over crystal streams, and a monastery ruin that occupied a majestic site before the power line came through.

We even saw some cyclists today. I think the cyclists must be smarter than we pedestrian pilgrims. They seem to have skipped the pass over the Pyrenees. They were all very polite.

Some had tiny cowbells hanging from the back of the bike to make their presence known; some had tiny horns that were not at all offensive; but most just used the universal pilgrim greeting:

"Buen Camino."

I'm glad I remembered from basketball practice that two pairs of socks help not to get blisters. So far, so good—at least as far as blisters.

Batou still is wearing me out. Today as I was lollygagging, she got way out in front again. The next mountain over. That was fine till I noticed the Sasquatch tracks and looked up to see it halfway between us moving toward her faster than I could move. As I started to run, I heard a bell but didn't think anything of it till a horse head had nudged between my legs and then lifted me up, sliding me down its mane until I was riding bareback.

That horse was fast. We flew over the stream, hooves never touching the stone slab bridge. Next thing I knew, the hooves were planted, neck was down, and I was sliding over the mane again, onto the back of

Sasquatch. But Sasquatch wasn't as willing as the horse. I rode him hard, spurring him in circles with my walking sticks, breaking him like a saddle horse. When he fell to his knees, I slid off his stinky back and was wondering what to do next when the horse reappeared and slung Sasquatch onto its back just as it had done me. In an instant they were gone, away from Batou, never to be seen again.

When I finally reached Batou, all she said was, "Where have you been? Tinkling behind that big tree?"

And of course I replied, "Yes, Dear."

Love,
Ba

ZUBIRI TO PAMPLONA

Dear R and G,

We were so tired last night we didn't even roll back the covers to check for bed bugs. We just climbed in and went to sleep. Do you remember the Cassis church bells? Same drill in Zubiri. Our room was down the street from the village church. I remember the 1:00 bell, then there were seven.

Day three might be the best day yet, but I am partial to three. I happen to know Aristotle had a fascination with the number three.

The image used for marking the trail is the yellow St. Jacque's clam or scallop, the Shell Oil Company logo minus the red. Many pilgrims hang a shell from their backpacks to distinguish themselves as pilgrims, but I'm pretty sure we are obvious.

The trail is well marked. In three days I've gotten off trail only once for a short distance before Batou reeled me back. At any rate, I'm looking forward to a bowl of those steamed clams once we get to Santiago de Compostela.

We started on flagstones, then moved on to a narrow trail canopied with fragrant wild roses, and eventually advanced to thistle-lined lanes. There were fields of grain, orchards, beautiful poppies, roosters crowing, cottonwood snow, and dogs barking.

We walked through a well-maintained magnesia plant early in the day.

Sometimes the grade was so steep we had to curve our toes downward to save our toenails.

For the most part the day was sunny and hot, but a few cool breezes did produce goose-bumps early on.

We took a respite on the Arga River, realizing Charlemagne and Napoleon had camped and Hemingway had fished for trout there.

We have eaten well here, even in the most modest places. Chicken here tastes like chicken; tomatoes taste like tomatoes. I could go on, but you get it.

Sixteen years ago, when you were merely glimmers in your mother's eyes, we rolled into Pamplona, a six-person family in a Fiat with five seatbelts. Brice didn't seem to mind being in the trunk, after we were almost refused entry into Spain. That's when Alexia discovered manchego cheese, that hard, Spanish cheese made from sheeps' milk, and Meggie discovered sangria, the refreshing table wine garnished with fruit and sometimes a little brandy or soda.

This morning we visited an abbey on the way and met a very interesting young man who has made it his mission to restore what is considered by many to be just another dilapidated church. The building was built in the Middle Ages by the Knights Templar. The footprint of the church is not the shape of a cross. It was a Christian church but had pagan symbols on the altar and a Jewish tree of life laid in stone into the entry way. The young man fears the restoration might take longer than his lifetime, but I am confident he will get 'er done. At any rate, it's my kind of church, and I urge you to see it someday.

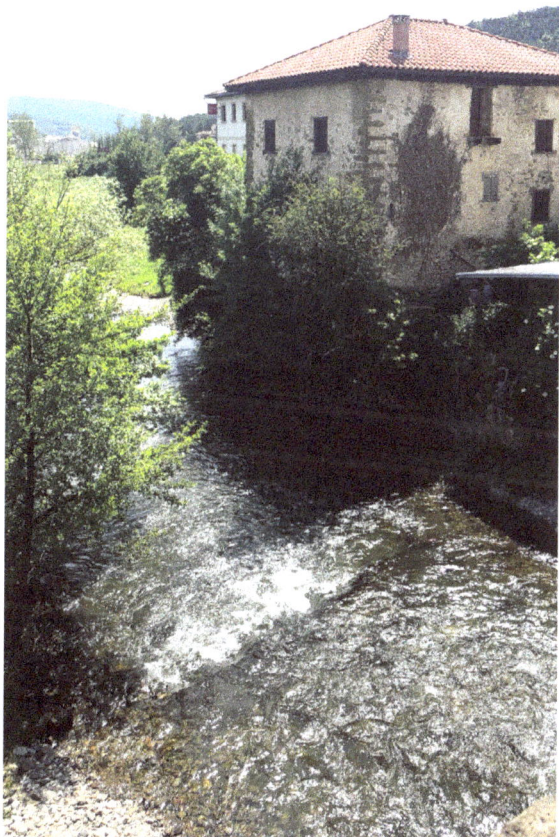

Three thoughts:

1. Don't pee on an electric fence.

2. When rationing water, drink less than half the remainder.

3a. It's "Yes, Ma'am" to your mother.

3b. Later it will be "Yes, Dear" to your wife.

Today Batou got so far in front of me I didn't know where she was. We weren't far from Arre, so I hoped she would wait for me there. She had earlier picked a huge bright red poppy and was wearing it on her hat like Yankee Doodle. I knew I'd be able to spot her, even in a crowd. There's a beautiful bridge over the River Arga at Arre. As I approached the town, I saw she had crossed to the other side of the river. The only problem was a huge mad bull on my side of the bridge, pawing his right hoof and getting ready to charge her. He had a ring in his nose that was as big as a door knocker and banderillas hanging from his neck like dreadlocks.

I'm going to share something with you that I've never told anyone else, not even Nonna and Pops. I've got some experience at bringing bulls to their knees. When I was in pee-wee league, I took a shortcut across a neighbor's field. I knew there was a bull there, but thought I could make it before he got to me from the barn. There was a swale in the field. As I walked down into it, he charged. There was no time to do anything but protect myself. I picked up and threw a rock instinctively and got a bullseye, or pretty close. That bull's knees fell like an old double-barrel opening. I ran and never looked back, convincing myself he'd be okay. I later understood the definition of irony when the neighbor came to visit, bringing us some hamburger that they didn't have room for in their freezer.

I picked up a river rock. There was no time for a spitball, no time to wind up. The bull was running away from me, toward Batou. I knuckled down and threw it as hard as I could, between the legs and floating upwards.

Now I have never scored below 100 on the golf course, but I know a good golf shot on the rare times I get one. It had the feel of a good shot. I got him in the family jewels.

He fell off the bridge, writhing down river, through the chute of the first falls, headed to Pamplona.

Batou had seen it all, so I was a little surprised at her nonchalant, "Dinner in three.

More. Miles."

"Splendid," I replied. "I've got a hankering for a little steak tartare."

There's some weather coming in from the west. Maybe I'll get a day off tomorrow.

Love,
Ba

PAMPLONA TO PUENTE DE LA REINA

Dear G and R,

There's more than one way to skin a cat.

When we got up at 7:00, it was raining cats and dogs, and both of us were feeling under the weather. It was an easy decision to sleep in.

Much of our way today would have been walking through the city of Pamplona, so Batou came up with a great plan—visit the Pamplona cathedral, taxi to our destination, then hike our route backwards, weather permitting, to see any sights we wanted to see.

The Pamplona Cathedral, built in the Middle Ages on top of an old Greek temple, is magnificent. To this day, the parishioners continue to unearth artifacts and to keep clean and maintain what they have. There were many beautiful things to see, but most striking were the silver, not gold, hanging

fixtures, the Turin bells, and an altar depicting Baby Jesus sitting on Joseph's lap instead of Mary's.

The village of Puente de la Reina, translated "bridge of the queen," population 2,200, is especially charming. The seven-arched (with two underground) Romanesque, stone bridge leading into town was built in the eleventh century by Queen Dona Estefania Mayor, especially for pilgrims.

By the way, each pilgrim is issued a pilgrim passport in which you collect stamps (sellos) along the way to certify you have made the trip. They are available from churches, inns, etc. Batou wonders if the French word "composter" might not have originated from this pilgrimage. The stamp used in Puente de la Reina is a depiction of the bridge.

Jacket weather today. The stampede straps saved our hats more than once.

I'm thinking of both of you, know you'll grow up to be courageous young men, and am regretting I'm missing a month of it.

I've come to realize the only time I'm faster than Batou is when I'm getting into the shade or into bed. Just heard ten bells. Got to get some rest so we can hit the road again tomorrow.

Love,
Ba

PUENTE DE LA REINA TO ESTELLA

Dear R and G,

We awakened to the hoots of owls, followed by the metronome click-clack of hikers on the cobblestones below our open window.

I am always appreciative of Batou and all she does for us and particularly grateful that, because of all the reservations she has made, we don't have to race other pilgrims to find our next room.

So, at nine bells, after we'd put more moleskin on our feet than our shoes at first would allow, we were off again.

I must admit I'm seeing so many churches that their details soon blur, so let me share what stood out to me at Puente de la Reina. First was the Moorish influence of the arch at the front door, followed by twenty-four-inch oak planks for flooring rather than some kind of stone. Then the lighting system

Batou discovered: near the exit there's a small, white metal box with a slot for a euro. Plug in a euro, and the interior electric lights come on for a few minutes, illuminating all kinds of shiny stuff we hadn't noticed before. We took our photos and then made it back to our pilgrim meal, which that night featured bull stew.

Something about TP. For a trail that's been around for over a thousand years, this trail is very clean, but it would be better not to see any tissues anywhere. Maybe Dr. Clark was right about those booster shots. I could write pages about the tissues here, the coarseness, scarcity, etc., but I won't. Suffice it to say that when hiking you should bring out what you bring in, or bury it.

The trail was less well marked today, but we managed. The flora and fauna are changing. We noticed huge slugs, edible snails, pines, old Roman roads, cumulus, nimbus, cirrus, and stratus all on the same blue pallet, poppy weeds in wheat fields, lemon trees, olive trees, grapes, wild asparagus that tasted like bitter weed, dry farmed vineyards tilled between the rows, and pharmacies filled with foot care products. My English teachers would be birthing cows about now.

We breathed in and spat out gnats.

We opened poppy buds just for fun.

Today it was the hat again. Batou picked a huge and fragrant genêts and wore it like a torch. Several commented she had the most beautiful hat on El Camino. Have you ever seen a flock of swallows flitting through the air like a school of fish? Think that but bees. They soon were swarming Batou with a vengeance.

Ever tried to save someone from a swarm of bees? The first thing I thought of was jumping into water. I did a 360, but nada. Yes, there was a clear puddle from yesterday's rain big enough for two lovebirds, but nothing else in sight. There was a wild rose hedge to the left, honeysuckle to the right. I pulled her into the honeysuckle as though I was about to kiss her for the first time, throwing the flower as far as I could back onto the path. We both did the breast stroke for a few feet then ran a small game trail a few more. Then we stopped dead still. All that could be

heard were our heartbeats and the swarm a few yards away, both growing quieter in a few moments. We soon were on the trail again, but not before another kiss.

Love,
Ba

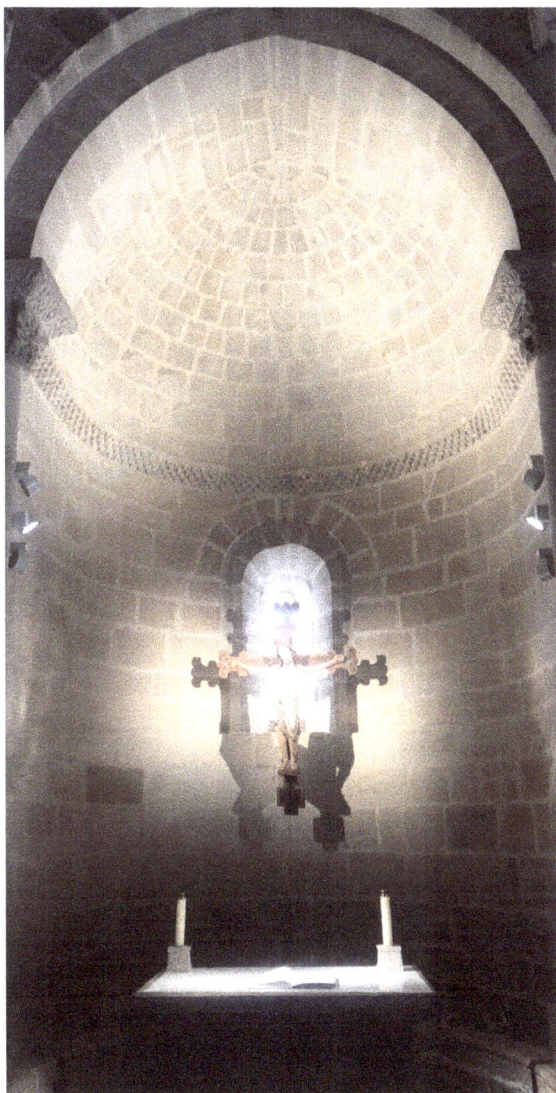

ESTELLA TO LOS ARCOS

Dear G and R,

It took traipsing a couple of villages to get the muscles stretched out and the blood and endorphins flowing today.

To quote Gandalf:

> The Road goes ever on and on down from the door where it began. Now far ahead the Road has gone, and I must follow, if I can, pursuing it with eager feet, until it joins some longer way where many paths and errands meet.

We walked past rock walls as high as Petit Jean Mountain. We saw beautiful vistas sometimes so bright that twice I was looking for my sunglasses before I realized I had them on.

We found at least one good reason for carrying a shell on the backpack. At the Bodegas

Irache Winery the company provides a taste of their wine from an outside spigot. Most pilgrims use their shells. Perplexed for just a moment, Batou suggested I empty my water bottle, pour us a taste, then refill the bottle at the water spigot, conveniently provided. By the way, there's plenty of potable water available on El Camino. I was overly prepared with two canteens; one is plenty.

Daisy petals. She loves me. She loves me not. She loves me. She loves me not. She loves me.

About halfway through our day, we decided to pull off the path for a picnic of manchego cheese, bananas, tonic water, and Tums under a beautiful eucalyptus tree. Batou was just a few yards in front of me and was reaching up to smell some low-hanging leaves when a black flash darted across the path and jumped onto her backpack, wrestling her into the ravine below as it clawed for the cheese. It was as big and fast as a panther, but I didn't think there were any panthers around here. It was a huge rat. What to do? I'd trapped rats before, but I didn't have much to work with and no time.

Normas de uso
A beber sin abusar
te invitamos con agrado,
para poderlo llevar
el vino ha de ser comprado.

Improvise. My leg muscles became the spring, and the titanium tip of a walking pole became the hammer. I jumped into the ravine and straddled the rat, putting my pole to his throat. I could have impaled him, but it would have been messy. I had half the cheese in my backpack, so I decided to negotiate. Fortunately, I have lots of experience negotiating with rats. There are many styles of negotiation, and you'll have to develop your own style. Some say always to demand more than you expect, and that's probably wise if you're forced to make the first offer. But I have found that rats respond better to bottom line demands. I said to the rat, "You take the cheese you've already clawed and leave Batou alone, or I'll run you through."

"Are you trying to threaten me?" screamed the rat.

"There's something you should know about me. I do what I say I'm going to do. I don't make threats."

"Wait, wait, wait. I don't want any more cheese—I just want out of the trap."

We had an accord. I pulled back on the pole, and the rat was gone. Batou and I shook ourselves off and found another spot for our half rations.

Love,
Ba

Los Arcos to Logroño

Dear Rhys and Garrison,

Today we saw ruins piled on ruins and wheat fields giving way to vineyards.

I usually could judge our direction by the way the rows of vineyards ran in relationship to the sun.

We rested under almond trees. We walked through villages getting ready for bull runs by barricading their route streets and helped the village of Viana celebrate its 800th anniversary.

I've adapted to be able to wrest and return my canteen from and back to my backpack on the run, and to holster my phone like Jack Nicholson in *Something's Gotta Give*.

I still have a geisha girl/moleskin hobble, but, as Brice might say, we've scheduled a zero day for tomorrow, so I'm thinking the toes

will get better. For lunch we stop at little food truck "bars" licensed along the way. Today we heard Proprietor Pepe tell of the pilgrim he had counseled who had lost her son in a tragic accident. She was, of course, devastated and was trying to cope by walking El Camino. Pepe said he ran his little stand because he loves people—that he had made his fortune long ago and that if he had to rely on the bar for his living, he'd starve. He said he'd talked to the woman the whole afternoon and had pointed out simple things—that when someone dies, the sun still comes up the next day, the seasons still change, life goes on. When she arrived in Santiago de Compostela, the pilgrim called Pepe to thank him and to let him know that on the final days of her trip, she'd felt her son was holding her hand.

Now for a story only Nonna knows. Back in the day I'd go with her to buy groceries. Her top three stores were Piggly Wiggly, Safeway, and Vickers' Market. We shopped sales and collected Gold Bond and Green Stamps. One day when I was about your age, I took a huge shiny red apple from the store without paying for it. When I climbed into the car, I put it between my legs because it was too big for my pockets.

"What's that?"

"An apple."

"Where'd you get it?"

"In the store."

"You come with me right now."

"Where are we going?"

"You're going to take that apple back to the manager and apologize."

"What's he going to do to me?"

"I don't know, and it doesn't matter."

I was scared. I thought I might go to reform school, but I took the apple back and handed it to the bewildered manager who looked at me then looked over my shoulder at my mother and nodded, an understanding nod that let me know I would not have to go to reform school, not then or ever, because I was too ashamed ever to do anything like that again.

Another day we were shopping multiple stores again. We'd bought a brown paper bag of cherries at Piggly Wiggly. Nonna pulled into the Safeway parking lot. "You stay here; I'll just be a minute." That was fine with me. The cherries were good. They were delicious. I ate the whole bag. Someday you'll go to a restaurant, get food poisoning, then never want to go to that restaurant again. That's the way I felt about cherries, until today. The low-hanging luscious cherries that hung over the trail today were so ripe that when Batou and I pulled on them, the red flesh separated from the pit right into our hands then into our mouths. I allowed myself three.

I almost forgot to tell you about the ghost. It happened first thing this morning. We were passing a cemetery while it still was dark. The Milky Way still was bright. We had gotten an early start because the distance for today was so far. I had approached the iron–latticed gate to the cemetery to see what I could see. There it was, an ephemeral blue body of a ghost, flitting over the graves like a butterfly—until it saw me. Then it came at me like a bullet. At first I thought the closed

gate would protect me, but the ghost came right through it. I threw one of my poles at it, and think I got a piece of it—but it kept coming. I used the other pole like a sword and cut off one of its arms—but it just grew three arms back. I sliced off its legs—then it morphed four more. I reconnoitered, looking over my shoulder to make sure Batou was okay. She was watching me and smiling, laughing really. I stepped back from the battle and said, "What?..."

"It's a cemetery gas. Methane. A will-o'-the wisp."

I'd been fighting a fart.

Love,
Ba

Day 8

LAYOVER IN LOGROÑO

Dear Garrison and Rhys,

Today we considered attitude. How to look at things. Positivity. Is your cup half empty, or half full? It's at least half full. My cup is brimming over, but the fuel tank is half empty. Be positive. Be prepared.

We saw a young man with ear buds listening to who knows what, oblivious to the world, cross a highway without looking in either direction. What happened to stop, look, and listen? I guess he was bored. I remember you didn't tell Mimi you were bored if you didn't want to be digging potatoes the rest of the day. Batou says she had to memorize poems if she dared to say she was bored.

Today we saw mountains taller than clouds, saw the oldest remaining Roman arches in Rioja, and learned an old Spanish saying about siesta—"Only cats and crazy people walk in the hot sun."

And we learned a little bit about wine. Remember the roses I planted at the ends of the rows of muscadines? I copied that from a little vineyard in Paris. Today I learned that roses are planted near vineyards because roses are even more susceptible to phylloxera than the vines are—like canaries in mines. I only planted the roses because I thought they were pretty.

And I had thought vintners didn't wash grapes before crushing them to save time and money. We were told today that if grapes are washed first, some of the natural yeasts necessary for fermentation are removed.

But that's boring. Let me tell you about lunch today. We found ourselves seated across the table from a lion with hazel eyes and a gun. He was formidable. How would you neutralize a lion with hazel eyes and a gun? I decided it best to try a smile and a disarming comment, but he ignored me the same way most cats do and continued staring at Batou and licking his lips. He started to growl. To distract him I looked at Batou and said, "Excuse me, Dear." Then I started to rise, but

in doing so I lifted our end of the table up with me and smashed the lion up against the wall. "There's about to be a ruckus."

I tied his hind legs with my belt like a roped calf, then we used the table cloth to tie his tail to the chandelier.

Then it was time to go.

We're now back at the hotel preparing for to-morrow. Who knows what it might bring? I'm hopeful, positive it will be good.

Love,
Ba

LOGROÑO TO NÁJERA

Dear Rhys and Garrison,

Pops once told me to figure three miles per hour for an average walk, and I had always found that to be about right, until today following Batou trying to outrun a rain storm, which we did with flying colors. I'm reminded of Papa who would look forward to going back to work so he could get some rest.

Leaving Logroño the trail was not well marked because of construction, but a very kind gentleman took us, Batou, really, under his wing and led us to the trail.

For my entire life I have avoided elevators for extra exercise, but for the last few days I'll ride them even when our room is on the first floor. Which is the second floor in the States, and don't forget: No floor thirteen.

Logroño would be a good sister city for Little Rock, about the same size.

Today we walked past granite picnic tables with benches and then small rock refuges where around 100 years ago vintners would sleep at night to protect the vineyards from those trying to steal the few healthy grape vines left after the phylloxera devastation. This is definitely wine country—Mediterranean climate, oats sown between rows to soak up too much moisture, rocky soils that look untillable, but well-tilled and manicured. There are over 600 vineyards in Logroño.

It was cool today.

We learned that pruned vine clippings make a great fire for grilling lamb chops, three minutes per side.

Today is the 500th anniversary of the women and children of Logroño surviving a seige of twenty-one days on nothing but what was available within the city walls—bread, fish, and wine—until the men came back from another battle to route the enemy. In the city center there's a massive medieval fair in celebration of that victory, and we were offered a slice of bread baked in a medieval oven set up in the plaza in commemoration.

We had lunch today at the edge of a very rocky vineyard. We leaned back against a stack of rocks so round they looked like cannon balls. As I stood up to stretch before taking off again, a metallic black and chrome motorcycle with two men on it approached in a very loud and menacing manner. "Hey old man, I smelled your stench from way back the road."

I didn't know what say to that, so I said nothing.

They both got off the bike.

One lit a cigarette, took a few puffs, then threw it at my feet. "You stink."

One pushed me over the pile of rocks while the other sneered at Batou. As I pulled myself up I had two rocks in my left hand and one in my right. Where to throw the first? I had a straight shot at the motorcycle and put a dent in the shiny gas tank that made it look as though a wrecking ball had gotten off course. The gas cap popped off. That gave me another idea. I picked up the burning cigarette.

"Amigo, amigo, we were just playing. We mean you no harm."

One picked up the gas cap and stripped it on. They both clambered on, and almost wrecked as they took off.

Batou put her pack on and said, "I trust you'll never buy a motorcycle."

"No, Ma'am."

Rhys and Garrison, never be a bully. Be kind.

And know this about bullies:

> Bullies are liars. They don't follow through.
>
> They only pick on people who won't fight back. If you fight back, you won't change their being a bully—they'll just go pick on someone else. You can trust me on this, it won't be you. I should probably stop here, and Mom might stop reading, but it's okay to wind up with a black eye dealing with a bully— just make sure he gets one too.

Love,
Ba

Logroño to
Santo Domingo de la Calzada

Dear Garrison and Rhys,

Pops used to joke about wearing his socks inside out because they were more comfortable that way. I did it that way today on purpose—and bought a pair of sandals. Everyone told me to use well broken in hiking shoes, not boots; and I did. I brought one pair so broken in they almost are worn out and for backup a second pair that felt great. The plan was to switch them out every other day. I used the newer ones a couple of days when we had a lot of climbing and descending, and now If you named me after my big toes, a good name would be Rudolph. Oh well, best to back up the backup.

Tonight we are staying in Parador Santo Domingo de la Calzada. It is just as exquisite as the parador we tried in Olite on that Pamplona trip I mentioned. It is an eleventh

century hospital built especially for pilgrims. Indeed, the town is celebrating this year its 1000th anniversary. My understanding is that paradors are national monuments that are restored, converted, and run by the Spanish government, with restrictions on the number of days you can stay, etc. Whoever's doing it, they're doing a great job.

Batou is the most determined and wonderful woman I have ever known. As I left Nájera this morning in a taxi in the rain, she was setting out on foot, backpack covered with the special rain proof cover she'd brought just for the occasion, umbrella in hand, concerned about my feet, although hers are probably worse, and the cold I'm still nursing. So, even though I have fresh cherries, truffles de vino, epsom salts, and extra moleskin awaiting her, I'm feeling guilty enjoying all this sumptuousness in this dining hall all to myself, this four-course lunch—"Excuso, mi esposa just called. Can you please set another place?"

Batou's photos of her hike today are good. Looks like vineyards gave out early on to potato and wheat fields, to wide open country with few trees.

This afternoon we took off to see the sights. Batou knew my toes were throbbing even though I'm now wearing sandals, so when the young man asked if she'd like to see the Grotto Hermoso, she said sure and then to me, "I'll be right back."

At first I planned to wait and rest, but something didn't feel right. I don't know if it was the name or the grammar, but Jimmy Stewart on his way to see the attraction in *How the West Was Won* came to mind. I followed them, vigilant for the accomplice, who appeared in a rush toward Batou, not suspecting me. I didn't have my sticks with me, but I can tell you that adrenaline is a better tool. I bopped one of them on the left ear, the other on the right so hard their heads butted each other. They blindly swung at me and hit each other. All that was left to do was the *coup de grace*—a swift kick in the butt to send them on their way to see the attraction themselves.

It's been another good day.

Love,
Ba

Santo Domingo to Belorado

Dear Rhys and Garrison,

Thirty-six degrees Fahrenheit and periwinkle skies this morning. Lots of jade colored eighteen-inch-high wheat and white poppies being cultivated. I tried to separate some of the wheat from the chaff with my teeth, but it's mostly chaff at this stage.

I started the day with four layers, never getting down to less than two. It was hot in the sun, but as I write this outside, I'm layering up again. There's a fire in the fireplace lobby of our hotel—first I've seen this trip.

There were lots of beautiful vistas today as we walked under lazy clouds blowing back to Navarre as we were entering the province of Castilla Y Leon.

I'm probably eating too many eggs on this trip, but the bright yellow yolks are visually appealing and delicious.

My favorite color is green. I was born on St. Patrick's Day, Gary Green Day. For years green was my color. Everything green. My name, my marketing, my clothes. When I started playing around with HeMan Tool Company, I chose colors of steel—blues, grays, black, etc. for the logo and everything else, including my clothes. I should have done it long ago—green is a harder color for me to work with clothes-wise. I must admit, however, that even now, when I wear a tie, I try to find one with a little green in it. At any rate, when I moved to mostly blues and grays, I realized they were on to something back in the 80's when a sales clerk would "do your colors." There's a lot to be said for not even thinking about buying something outside that range. I've got too much stuff, so being able to pass up a beautifully designed quality green item, even if it costs only a penny was a good filter for me.

All of that to say that I didn't think anything of the color of the soles of my copper-lined, stink-free, red and orange boot socks that now announce I am wearing sandals. By the way, these hiking sandals so far seem to be the bomb. I pick up a few beggar lice on my socks and a few pebbles under my arches, but the toes feel much better.

This morning as we were walking through the first village of the day, I passed an elderly lady's door just as she was opening it. Realizing she was startled and not wanting to frighten her further, I smiled and said, "Buenas dias." About five strides farther down the street I heard:

"Buen Camino,"

and looked over my shoulder to see her smiling and waving as though we were kin.

This afternoon as El Camino paralleled the highway for a while, a trucker shouted.

"What did he call me?" I bristled. Batou gave me the evil eye.

He said:

"Buen Camino."

I told Batou she wasn't eating enough.

This afternoon a cold and blinding wind wrapped her stampede strap around her head in a figure eight, popped open the umbrella attached to her pack, and lifted her like Mary Poppins, except completely out of control. The only good thing I noticed is that there were no power lines in sight. She swirled and swirled high in the sky until her stampede strap caught on a bell tower weather vane. When she finally cut free from that, she plopped right on her bottom into a nest. There she was, sitting in what looked like an eagle aerie, except she was clamoring around with a bunch of stork chicks. And they were excited. It sounded like the drum of a bunch of woodpeckers. Papa stork flew away. Mama stork circled a couple of times then lit on the nest, wings spread around Batou and all the other chicks. The chicks calmed down. Mama stork closed her wings and settled in as though there was nothing wrong. Batou looked down at me and screamed, "Help."

As you might imagine storks build their nests in hard to reach places. I don't know what their natural predators are, but I'll bet you they fly.

I ran around the bell tower. There was a door. Of course it was locked, and of course it was siesta. The only two people in sight were Batou and me.

I ran away from the tower to get a better perspective, never taking my eyes off Batou. Suddenly there was a shadow and a swoop that hunkered me down. Papa stork flapped his wings around me just as mama stork had done to Batou. I hunkered down even more, but the wings flapped even faster and then he was gone, the jacket that had been wrapped around my shoulders in his beak.

There was then the same commotion at the nest—papa stork flapping, Batou screaming for help, and I was still running around the bell tower, looking for a ladder, trying to come up with a plan.

Then came again the shadow and the swoop. This time the flutter was only a hover, just long enough to drop into my arms a neatly bow-tied jacket with my baby swaddled inside.

"Grassy ass, Senior Stork. I happen to have a tin of sardines in my backpack. Will you please take them for your family as a token of my appreciation?"

"De nada, amigo:

Buen Camino."

Love,
Ba

BELORADO TO ATAPUERTA

Dear Garrison and Rhys,

Today was like going to the gym, four times. Batou walked the entire distance. I hailed a taxi the last mile and a half because my feet told me to. We started the day with possum socks and gloves. Now it's pleasant in the shade.

We walked through a herd of cows, bulls, and calves with no incident. They were too busy chewing their cud to worry about us.

People talk about losing weight on El Camino because of all the walking. I haven't noticed that for either Batou or me, but Batou says my money belt is cinching in.

Batou purchased an app that gives a lot of information to those who would use it. I'd say about ten percent of the monument markers are written in Spanish, French, and English; the rest are Spanish only.

I noticed a message in a baggie today, paper weighted down with a bright green rock on El Camino outside Villagranca Montes de Oca: "Cathy Thompson from San Diego please contact home urgently."

Today Batou saved me. I was following a deep sandy gulley, noticing all kinds of interesting rocks that recently had been exposed by all the rains and snow melt. A rock shaped like a heart caught my eye. I couldn't tell if it had been shaped by nature or by man, but I knew Batou would love it. As I reached to pick it up, the whole gulley collapsed, and I went sliding down the hill like Michael Douglas in *Romancing the Stone*. The only difference was that I landed in quicksand. Pops taught me that the more you struggle the quicker you sink, so I tried to remain calm. I'd heard to try to crawl out on your belly, but I already was up to my waist. I also knew that when you find yourself up to your neck in poop to stop talking, to plead the fifth. I didn't have much time. "Batou, Batou."

You might not know this, but Batou can hear a gnat fart. She was there in an instant. She held onto a tree trunk and reached out for

me. No way. She tied her two poles together and slung them toward me. Not enough. I threw her my poles. She tied them all together. Still not enough. Two feet short. I threw her my belt. Just in time she had it all tied together and cast the conglomeration to me like she was fly fishing. I caught the belt. She pulled and pulled until I was out of the muck.

"Let's stay on trail from now on."

"Yes, Dear."

Love,
Ba

ATAPUERTA TO BURGOS

Dear Boys,

We left Atapuerta to the sound of cocks crowing and bleating sheep, marveling at the cool mountain mist that turned out to be limestone smog from an industrial plant, we realized once we reached the downhill.

It was jacket weather up the hill, shirt sleeves by the way down.

The inn last night was lovely, probably the oldest we've stayed in, and that's saying a lot. I reckon the hand-hewn beam I bumped my head on this morning to be around 800 years old.

On the way into Burgos El Camino merged with a new highway. It was a pity, really. Cobblestones covered with pavement. The contractor left about eighteen inches of cobblestones on the outside lane. For old time's sake, Batou walked the cobblestones; for old soles' sake, I walked the macadam.

As we were approaching an extremely busy intersection on the highway, a lorry driver saw us and abruptly stopped for us to cross, backing up a lot of cars in a hurry. As I looked up to nod appreciation, I noticed the inside of his cavernous cab was designed as though a cathedral. I swear. I know that twelve miles in the Spanish sun causes some to tilt at windmills. I wish there had been time for a photo.

This morning two paths diverged out of Atapuerta both with yellow shell signs; we took the path with less sheep poop. We noticed it was the road less traveled and later from the sheep herder understood why. NATO rounds were exploding nearby. At first machine guns, and then what sounded like Lugers. We ran back toward the other path only to run into double rows of barbed wire, somewhat like the electric fence around the vineyard—if the first fence row doesn't get you, the second one will.

The sheep herder told Batou, "I don't know why they put up that second sign last

week—that path takes you through the military zone."

Boys, for all I talk about guns, and sword fights, and throwing rocks, I want you to know I go out of my way not to step on a bug, not even an asp worm, one of which stung me when I was about your age and which I'll never forget.

Love,
Ba

PROHIBIDO
EL PASO
ZONA MILITAR

BURGOS TO HORNILLOS

Dear Rhys and Garrison,

Last night we enjoyed the best pork knuckles I've ever eaten—meat removed from the bone, cooked with carmelized onions and fresh mushrooms. Some people probably think sopping with bread is uncouth, but I meant it as a compliment to the chef.

Montana has nothing on this big sky. And Austin has less limestone. The dirt in the fields, mostly wheat and oats now, is literally white.

Have you ever passed cars and trucks on a freeway, only to have them pass you later, then back and forth passing each other for a long time? That's how the trail was with pilgrims, especially today. I feel as if I know several of them, even though the extent of conversation for the most part has been:

"Buen Camino."

This morning we stopped in a small church in a very small village. By the way, Batou never passes a church she doesn't try to enter. Many are closed except at certain times. She loves the architecture, history, and spirituality. I took off my hat, and Batou made her sign of the cross as we entered. I didn't see anyone else in the church. I sat on the last pew and took a photo of the pretty altar. As we started to leave we noticed two nuns sitting in the corner. They stood to greet us, explaining they lived in a little house in the village and that it was their mission to take care of the church and any pilgrims in need. One of them asked if she could put a token of Mother Mary around our necks on a string necklace to protect us on our journey. Of course we accepted; and I still have it on; and there's no telling how much money Batou left in the offering plate upon our departure.

When the nun put the token around my neck, she gave me one of those friendly kisses Europeans use that sometimes can be awkward for me, at least, without practice. It's right cheek to right cheek, then left cheek to left cheek; voila.

By the way, Kimi would like the room we're staying in tonight. Each room in the inn named by a color. Ours is lilas. I'd call it very purple.

Perhaps you've noticed that many manhole covers are cast with the name of the foundry on them, or sometimes with a picture of something representative of a community. In Arkansas some have a razorback. We walked through a town that had mulberry bushes on some of the manhole covers. As I was hustling to catch up with Batou, one of my walking stick tips slipped into the finger hole of one of the manhole covers. The stick was securely strapped to my wrist. Just before that, a nice neighborhood cat had taken a liking to me. I might need to throw away that tin of sardines. The cat was rubbing against the inside of my leg the way cats sometimes do.

It's rather a blur. I'm walking fast. There's a cat wrapped around my leg. My stick anchors itself in an iron manhole cover, and I do a 360 or two before I can slow down enough to extricate myself from the silly situation. Batou hears the commotion, thinks the cat is a

weasel, comes back to pop it off my leg, and I've been singing that silly song in my head ever since.

Love,
Ba

HORNILLOS TO CASTROJERIZ

Dear Garrison and Rhys,

Please tell your dad, "Happy Fathers' Day."

As we entered the dining room last night there was an Irish couple singing along to the background music, "Country Roads." As the proprietor seated us he asked, "Te gusta?" We replied, "Si." For the rest of the evening, nothing but John Denver songs. A little John Denver goes a long way.

In the long shadows of the morning we started up a hill and could see above the tree tops only the white end tips of scores of windmill blades, white whirling dervishes dancing across the horizon.

It is possible James Taylor chose deep greens and blues while on this walk, along these wheat fields under this sky, but probably he was looking at pines.

Batou got in front of me again today. I had stopped to take a photo. I noticed her stoop as she approached a cattle guard crossing.

I later learned a snake had asked Batou to carry it to the other side of the hot metal crossing, and she had obliged. As soon as they safely were across, the snake bit her.

"Why did you do that?" she screamed. "Because I'm a snake," it replied.

As far as I'm concerned there are two kinds of snakes, good ones and bad ones, rounded heads and triangular heads, non-venomous and venomous, but all best to be left alone. I understand that here, or at least in France and Spain, there are two types. Vipers, which are venomous, and *couleuvre*, non-venomous.

I took the snake's head to the doctor. Batou put her blistered feet on the exam table. "My gosh, this is serious, but I think she'll be okay as soon as the swelling goes down," the doctor said. "Now let's take a look at that snake bite."

Love,
Ba

CASTROJERIZ TO FROMISTA

Dear Rhys and Garrison,

The street engineers of these villages must have begun with a building here, a building there, a garden plot there, and then connected everything as best they could. It's a hodge podge; left, right, left, right, left; and then we are on our way.

It's now drier and hotter. Everything irrigated. The wheat is ripe and now tastes like breakfast.

The flora has changed a bit. The fauna sounds alongside the canal we walked today were a symphony.

When driving a dusty road it is kind to slow down near pedestrians, to keep the dust down as much as possible.

Today was dreamy hot. During the short shadows I saw a dragon in the distance;

pyramids became bales of hay; x-ray clouds revealed dots of doom from the dogs of war.

I am planning my next cross examination.

I heard boots close behind. I hurried to get away, to catch up to Batou. I reconnoitered to the right and got kicked from the left. When I turned to the left, adrenaline flowing, somehow the poles got between my legs in the loose gravel. Then I got kicked from the right as I began tumbling toward Batou. When I regained consciousness, I asked, "Who was after us?"

I got the look.

"It must have been the extra set of boots banging behind your backpack."

Love,
Ba

FROMISTA TO
CARRION DE LOS CONDES

Dear Garrison and Rhys,

We've enjoyed nice dinners since I mentioned the knuckles. Last night what stuck out for me was the pan-seared cylinder of brie atop the green salad. The night before, we both enjoyed fresh fried anchovies.

I can't say we've had a bad dinner, but bread and water would taste pretty good after all this walking.

Cuckoos cuckooing, roosters ci ci ricing, and wind howling, we set off this morning to blue sky.

We stopped to admire and to try to capture photos of undulating wheat fields jigsawed by the wind and honeycomb-textured by fleeting cloud shadows.

Kilometers don't take as long, and euros don't last as long either. We're now down to less than 400 kilometers to Santiago de Compostela.

Use all the sun screen you want, especially on the face, hands, and ears; but clothing is the best protection from the blistering sun.

Today was a doozy. Batou got two miles in front of me. I had stopped to smell and water the roses, take a photo, etc. It was about a mile to where we needed to turn right to get to our parador, and she already had made the turn. I could see her pretty hat speck in the distance, and I could see the parador way off to the right. A lowrider drove past me, music blaring and shouting insults which I'm certain did not include:

"Buen Camino."

Sticks and stones can break my bones, but words can never hurt me, so I didn't give them a second thought—until they turned right. Then it was time to do something, even if it was wrong.

But what? I had wind and wheat to work with.

I took off my hat, tied the stampede string to the end of one of my poles and took off. My sandals slid over those wheat crowns as though they were ball bearings. I used the other pole as a tiller when I needed to make corrections.

It was fun, but I was on a mission—to reach the lowrider before the lowrider reached Batou.

People who did better at math than I could have figured exactly when and where point of impact would be, but I was just going by feel and knew I would get there come hell or high wind—come on wind. And it did. It quickly became obvious I was going to cut them off.

And I had the element of surprise on my side. They hadn't connected me with Batou, her being so far in front of me and all.

I just needed a plan once I landed.

Of course, I don't know what they were thinking—I almost overshot them, but I didn't. I landed right where I intended to, pretty much. Right on top the roof of the lowrider.

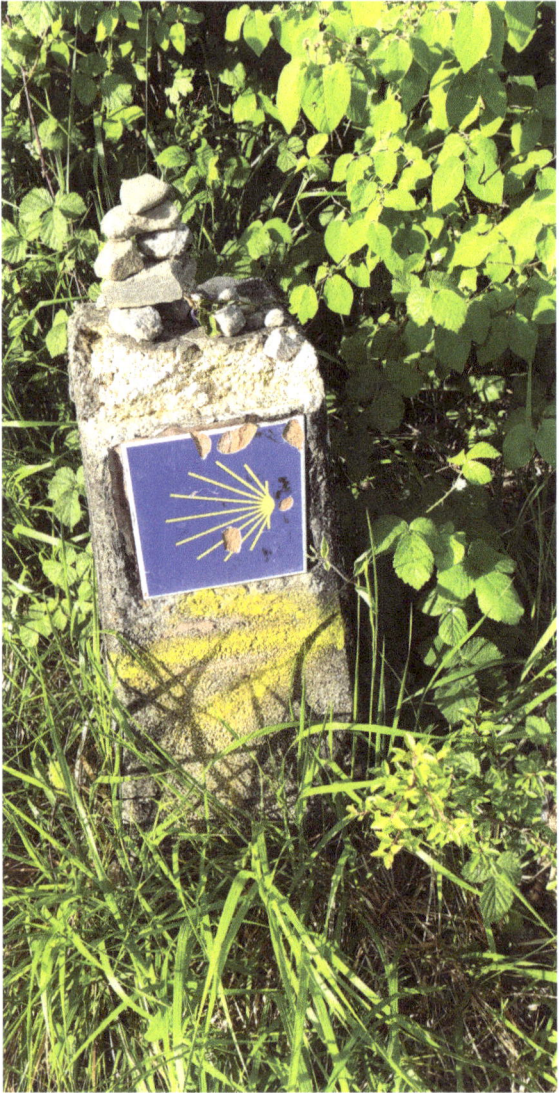

"Ándale, ándale," I shouted as I used the tiller pole as a whip. And they obliged. I knew from my study of body language the fight was over. They looked at me as though I were a madman and drove faster and faster, trying to shake me.

We passed Batou, then we passed the inn, then I figured it was time to let up on the whip and glide off.

As I approached the inn from the opposite direction, Batou was just arriving. "Where have you been?"

"Sorry, My Sweet. I got so far behind I had to take the shortcut."

Love,
Ba

CARRION DE LOS CONDES
TO CALZADILLA DE LA CUEZA

Dear Rhys and Garrison,

Last night at the parador monastery, enjoying haute cuisine beneath hundred-foot-long and thousand-year-old rafters, I asked Batou, "Seriously, why did you want to make this trip? Did the nuns at your school lock you in the cellar till you promised? I know you say you've been wanting to do this for years, but why, really?"

She looked at me and smiled, knowing after all these years that I have Southern white male syndrome and a badly timed sense of humor that is well intentioned but that sometimes is misunderstood as flippant, or worse, uncaring.

"I wanted to come here because I love to travel, love learning about new things. I love the history, the culture, the people. I love the feeling of spirituality. I love doing things that are difficult; I enjoy the satisfaction of completing a difficult task. I love to hike. I love the adventure.

What about you?"

"You know when you pull the covers back at night to check for bed bugs? I want to be there every night, forever—because someone's got to pull back those covers for me."

When we checked into the inn this evening, I was exhausted. I threw my pack on the floor, opened the shutters and windows, took from my pockets the two rocks that I've been carrying with me since the bull fight. The plan was to bring one to each of you as a souvenir. They were the same size and color. I thought you might use them to play marbles or boulles. I put them on the night stand.

Maybe I rested my eyes.

I remember awakening to the whoosh of drones. Flitting and buzzing everywhere. Peeping on my privacy. Recording without my permission. The first rock sent one spiraling toward the terrace below. If you practice your whistle by pressing your lips tightly

together and exhaling for a long time you can imagine the sound it made before crashing. The second rock missed, but the whoosh it made sucked the second drone out with it. Still, there were more. I ran to the bathroom to wet one end of a towel so that I could bullwhip them into submission.

Then I heard the "Whoa, whoa, whoa.

Why don't you go on down to dinner? I'll be there in just a few minutes."

And a few minutes later there she was, looking radiant as always, and wearing a most fragrant new perfume—rosemary and clove.

Later in the room it smelled as though she must have spilled the perfume bottle. It smelled great, but best of all, there were no more drones.

Love,
Ba

Calzadilla de la Cueza to La Cordoniz Sahagun

Dear Garrison and Rhys,

'Twas a long but good day. We raced the rain and won. We are at the hotel now. A very old building with good bones. This hotel is a good example of the Mudéjar style of architecture, which, in Arabic, stands for the ones left behind, the leftovers or remnants of the Moors dispersed by the Christians in the Middle Ages who stayed and influenced architecture and culture alongside Christian architecture and culture.

El Camino is beautiful in its spring splendor, but you can see all kinds of buds about to break to make a beautiful summer, as well. Not as many small farms; more thousand-acre wheat fields; fewer poppy weeds in the well-managed and clean farms.

Moving every day, I've decided to wash clothes every day rather than lug dirty clothes.

Washing them in the sink or tub, wringing them a time or two, and then finding a place to hang them till the next morning takes about half an hour, significant over any period of time.

I am reminded of the first washers I can remember, a vast improvement over the scrub boards the previous generation dealt with. The first one I recall was so messy we used it outside, in the carport area. The washer/agitator was electric, but that was it; no rinse or spin cycle; no dryer. There might have been a top on the washer, but I don't think so. I recall a hand-operated wringer attachment and the admonition not to get your teat caught in the wringer.

Clothes were wrung into elevated, castor-wheeled tubs of rinse water filled from a water hose, then repeated into a second rinse tub and then wrung into baskets before being taken to the clothes line, shaken out, and hung with clothes pins to dry in the wind and sun.

I recall babies being bathed in the second rinse water before it was dumped onto the grass. If you ever hear "threw the baby out with the bath water," I wanted you to have a reference.

By the way, there are many more clothes lines here than in the U.S. But their state of the art washers and dryers are more sophisticated, more powerful because of the voltage. The spin cycles here operate at such high RPM that dryers really aren't needed.

Batou says the left side of my face is more freckled than the right, but everything exposed is pretty blotchy.

Love,
Ba

La Cordoniz Sahagun
to El Burgo Ranero

Dear Rhys and Garrison,

It certainly seems like the longest day of the year.

Early this morning we overshot our trailhead by around a quarter mile. I mistakenly thought Batou was wanting to backtrack to take a longer, more scenic route. I told her she could take the French route if she wanted to, but my back didn't feel like backtracking. So we parted ways for the day. Cut to the chase— when I got to the hotel she had beaten me by an hour. And worst of all, I had not practiced what I preach, had not said, "Yes, Dear," even when it was in my best interest.

Batou says I am stubborn, and I resemble that remark.

Along my lonely way I communed with the cuckoos and field rats. The rats cried at my

countenance, and the cuckoos kept saying all day, "Cuckoo, cuckoo, cuckoo."

A walk by a group of goats today brought back an old memory of when we had owned a goat for few days. When we moved to where Nonna and Pops live, we'd dug a water well to supply the house. I recall Papa using his witching sticks to find the best places to drill for water, which happened to be next to the houses. There was a large pile of soil and clay near our house from the well digging, and somehow we had gotten a goat. The goat loved to play King of the Mountain on that little hill. One morning as we were leaving for church, the goat was on top of the hood of our car. When we got home, the goat was gone.

All well here. Batou says, "Hola."

Love,
Ba

El Burgo Ranero
to Mansilla de las Mulas

Dear Rhys and Garrison,

For some reason Batou didn't want to let me out of her sight today.

We walked and talked about all sorts of things.

I already knew about oil of clove for a tooth ache in an emergency, but until the drones, I'd never realized clove and rosemary could be so effective in repelling flies.

Last night I tried arnica for aching muscles, and it seemed to work.

Tonight I plan to run a needle and thread through a blister, then leave the thread in for the rest of the night. That's a remedy Batou learned from her great-grandfather.

Batou did a little research recently for blister remedies. Strong suggestion numero uno

was to "Cease immediately the activity that is causing the blister." She decided to seek another opinion.

Something to realize early on is that the world does not always make sense. By the way, this statement, even though it follows a paragraph about second opinions, has nothing to do with second opinions. It is an attempt to sum up world events in a single sentence.

As we passed mile ten today I was tired and looking to escape Batou's loving, watchful eye. It came in the curve just after we'd passed over a stream. Her steps quickened, much like a pony approaching the barn. I emptied my canteens, made sure the tops were on tight, threw them in the backpack for extra buoyancy then jumped in. I floated, exerting no energy, enjoying those last laps in a most luxurious way. When I walked out of the water I was approached by a waiter wearing a white apron, carrying a silver tray on which set a huge tumbler with ice cubes as big as eggs. "For you, Señor, lemonade and tonic, shaken, not stirred."

"Of course. Grassy ass."

"Anything else, Señor?"

"Si, por favor. Donkey banjo?"

Love,
Ba

MANSILLA DE LAS MULAS TO LEON

Dear Garrison and Rhys,

Barren and hot. Just another day with my idle thoughts and the woman of my dreams.

Our dinner table last night was an antique threshing board, a huge slab of wood impregnated with pebbles, pulled by an ox, used to separate grains from their straws—similar to the wash board I mentioned but much larger. This one was covered with glass.

I never had a pet pig, but we did raise a pig for bacon when I was a very young boy. I remember slopping it with a dusty something mixed with water and whatever leftovers there might have been. My recollection is a pig will eat anything. I remember the day the pig went away but not much more about it.

I never took an economics course, and I'm sure it shows, but I can tell you that it's usually easier, less expensive, and makes

more sense to hire it done than do it your-self, even if you are a jack of all trades.

I now will discuss something more because of my age than yours, a career. Having reached the age where I could retire if I wanted to, I'd like to share with you what I've learned.

- Do what you love.

- Love what you do.

- Do what you're good at and can make a living that suits you.

- Do it as well you can.

- Do something that helps people.

It's okay to love eating popsicles but hard to make a living at it. If you decide to be a pig farmer, that's fine with me. Just do it well. Raise the best pigs in the country. If that's what you want to do, I'll help you plant the best oak trees for the best acorns for pigs. Your hams could rival the Spanish ham I've become so fond of over here. If that's what you want to do. Love what you do, do it very well, and rely on others to help with almost everything else. Realize that everyone has to make a living, and that what you do is no more or less important than what anyone else does.

By the way, I never intend to retire as long as I have my health. I love what I do. I know I help others. I darned sure need to call on them for almost everything else. And forty days and forty nights pilgrimages aren't free.

As we entered the old walled area of Leon today, the first wall Roman, the second medieval, I lifted my sticks high above my head in an attempt to stretch back into place my sciatic nerve.

A passing Spaniard saw me and asked, "Rocky Balboa?"

"Si, Señor."

Love,
Ba

Leon to Mazarife

Dear Rhys and Garrison,

It's been raining all day. I'm now sitting beside a fireplace at our bed and breakfast. I enjoy stoking the fire.

Our hotel last night in Leon was in the monarchial palace on which construction began in the year 1015. As we toured the crypt, the tour guide told us that of all the coffins there, only three were spared damage by Napoleon's troops. When I mentioned to Batou it might be time for a new piece of art above our fireplace she said, "I tried to tell you."

Today is a Spanish national holiday. We heard fireworks last night till after midnight.

The fireworks reminded me of my first business failure. A neighbor friend had asked his father for money to buy fireworks. His father's reply was that he'd buy enough fireworks for a stand on the highway in front of my friend's house. I was approached to help set up and staff the stand. After doing my share of the work in setting up, and after only one hot afternoon of slack sales, my friend took a punk, lit it, and then proceeded to set off every piece of inventory we had. We stayed friends for a while, but my first business with a partner was a bust.

Later, as I would drive home from college, I would stop to visit Pop's mom, your great-great-grandmother, who advised me that the only bad thing about failure was not to get back up, and to be wary of business partners. Friends have taught me that successful people fix their mistakes. We all make mistakes. And one good friend shared something his mom taught him as a young boy. "Take small bites—in case a pretty girl walks up to you at lunch and wants to talk, you don't want to be talking with a mouthful of food."

Know what is important.

Love,
Ba

MAZARIFE/VILLAVANTE TO ASTORGA

Dear Garrison and Rhys,

The rain in Spain falls mainly on the plain, and did so today for the last couple hours of our walk.

My hands suggest I'm a Navaho elder; my feet would get me kicked out of a spa.

When I say I'm working in the fields, there's a lot of lollygagging involved; I think when Batou goes to the gym, she really works out. She's hard to keep up with.

I'm working this trail like a rented mule. Indeed, last night at our inn were three caballeros who are riding El Camino on horseback. They take an extra horse with them and make about thirty kilometers a day. So far our maximum daily distance has been twenty-eight klicks—we do have a thirty-one on the horizon.

I saw ants carrying wheat into their mound today.

In 1986, our host town, Astorga, celebrated its 2000th year.

It's after 10 P.M., and it's still light outside.

Good night.

Love,
Ba

Astorga to Rabanal del Camino

Dear Rhys and Garrison,

Another day, another twenty-one kilometers.

Long day because we left Astorga late, after viewing the palace designed by Gaudi—such a tremendous modern architect to have lived so long ago.

As we left Astorga, we passed acre after acre of old stone ruins. We discussed what they might have been—maybe just rock enclosures for animals, maybe Roman suburbs abandoned after Astorga was no longer a Roman garrison. Maybe I'll get around to more research someday, but for now just know we saw a lot of Roman and medieval rock walls, all the timbers, if any ever there were, long gone, crying out for preservation.

Add tea tree oil to the list of folk remedies good for blisters.

I have drunk from over fifty community water spigots from France to here, and no problems yet.

If I mentioned European recycling before, please forgive me. I try not to repeat myself, but we are keeping a hectic schedule. Things do start to run together. At any rate, they are beating us hands down—color coded, convenient, and the only way to get rid of your trash.

Speaking of hectic schedule, it's after 11 P.M., and we've just finished dinner and washing clothes, and plan a 7 A.M. departure over the mountains again tomorrow—nineteen miles.

I've worn nothing but sandals and socks on my feet for the last week.

Have you ever tried to ride a large iguana? Don't waste your time.

Unusual for me, I was walking about a quarter mile ahead of Batou today. I had just passed a huge iguana sunning on a rock and was wondering how to harness it. We were the only pilgrims still on the isolated country

road because of our late departure. A van with a side door passed me and didn't slow down, but I noticed as it rolled toward Batou the brake lights came on. I decided I needed to get back there in a hurry. I lassoed the iguana with the pole strap of one of my sticks and jumped on its back.

Big mistake, as it just went round in circles trying to bite me. I jumped off the side away from its teeth, held onto the pole end as a leash and used the other pole as a whip. It was like being pulled by Zelda, but much faster. If I needed it to go right, I whipped the left tail; if I needed to go left, I whipped the right tail. We zig-zagged, but as two hombres jumped out of the side of the van intent upon Batou, the snarling iguana already was within their peripheral vision.

Batou took off her backpack and threw it at the hombres as though it were a bomb. But by then they were averted to the iguana racing toward them with a crazy man whipping left and right. Batou pulled out her knife and headed to the pine thicket. The hombres scrambled back into the van, and it peeled out down the highway. I let go the iguana.

Batou came out of the thicket, picked up her pack, and said, "Let's get to the hotel—it's been a long day."

Indeed it had, but tomorrow promises to be even longer.

Will keep you posted.

Love,
Ba

Rabanal del Camino to Ponferrada

Dear Garrison and Rhys,

It was hot today, but usually there was a good breeze to keep the drones away. It was so hot pigs and cows were sharing the same shade trees.

We saw lots of slate. Went through one village where every roof was black slate. We saw slate that looked like petrified wood, walked over slate that crumbled at the touch, slate that had been cut with saws, and slate that had been backhoed. When we checked into our hotel, there were three huge slabs of slate used for blackboard messages—reminded me of when I was in elementary school and it being an honor to be asked by the teacher to take the chalk erasers to the basement and clean them on the grindstone-like brushes. It was either that or stay in class. We kept those brushes clean.

El Camino has been good for me.

Today I worked on anger management. A rude motorist almost ran me over, and my first reaction was to violence. I am lucky it turned out to be like the dog chasing the car and not knowing what he'd do if he caught it. It took me a while to calm down, but I remembered the need to count to ten, at least, before reacting. Resorting to violence is a reaction, not a choice. A good choice is to remain calm. As soon as it happened, I noticed proverbs written on rocks, "Live in the moment; the trail is wider when you smile; with each breath we grow closer to death, so live in the moment, enjoy every breath."

Always stay calm.

Love,
Ba

PONFERRADA TO VILLAFRANCA DEL BIERZO

Dear Rhys and Garrison,

I forgot to mention a couple things: "hobbit houses" built into sides of hills along the way; some still used but mostly abandoned. The ones we read about mentioned tools inside that dated to the fifth century.

And last night we toured what I understand to be the oldest remaining Knights Templar castle—certainly the oldest and biggest castle I remember seeing that wasn't a ruin. Built during the first iron age. Catapults, cannons, and cross bows on display, as well as a beautiful library. By the way, always be straight as an arrow; a crooked arrow cannot be true.

Trails continue to be perilous downhill mountain paths to pattern-tiled sidewalks, and everything in between.

It's been hot and sunny. We're back in grape country, but not as fancy as Rioja country—lots of abandoned vineyards. Here the most prevalent grape is Menci'a.

Lunch today in Cacabelos—no idea about the origin of that name.

Tonight another parador. Yea.

We hit the less-than-200-kilometers-mark today.

Batou sends her love.

Love,
Ba

VILLAFRANCA DEL BIERZO
TO HERRERIAS

Dear Garrison and Rhys,

Nobody ever accused me of thinking too fast. After four weeks on the trail I have decided I'm a half-day guy. When I play golf, which is seldom since planting muscadines, I'm a nine-holer. If ever I were to run a marathon, which is not likely, I assure you it would be a half marathon, but winners never quit, and quitters never win, so I'll just switch tack. Over 600 klicks into an 800 klick deal, and I'm changing the way I do things. I'll walk with Batou till she calls lunch; we'll have a nice lunch; then she can beat to port; I'll tack to a taxi. Batou says she enjoyed the solace of the trail this afternoon; I enjoyed practicing my Spanish, "Taxi, por favor. Siesta."

Did I tell you about pilgrim meals?

Almost every eatery along the way offers a three-course meal for a reasonable price, at

AXI MOLINASEC

LUIS

+34 671 708 07

ATENCIÓN ESPECIAL AL PEREGRI

TAXIS MOLINASECA

FÉLIX

4 y 7 PLAZAS

(+34) 681 200 466

Se aceptan tarjetas de Crédito

least less expensive than the a la carte menu. Our experience is they've been pretty darned good.

I've been doing a lot of walking but can't say I've lost any weight. In four weeks we've been disappointed with the food maybe twice. Those are good odds, even where I speak the language.

When you show your Pilgrim's Passport, you get significant discounts into museums, etc. Night before last I forgot to take my Pilgrim's Passport to the Knights Templar castle, but offered to show the sales clerk my feet to prove I was a pilgrim; she was not impressed.

At our inn for tonight, they are baling hay while the sun shines. When at 2 P.M. I baled to a taxi, the thermometer in the taxi read thirty-five degrees Celsius.

In 2013, I was working the vines in high heat. I got so hot I almost fell to my knees. I made my way back to the car in case I passed out—figured that was the safest place. I sat in the shade with the AC running for a few minutes. It passed. I recall the same thing happening to Papa—all those who loved him

were overly concerned. He lived another thirty years after that. I share this in case it ever happens to you, and encourage you to get out of the sun during high temperatures.

Love,
Ba

HERRERIAS TO O CEBREIRO

Dear Rhys and Garrison,

I'll start with a couple of Jefferson quotes, but not verbatim:

"It's acceptable to prune one's fig tree to be able to stand under its shade." But I've not yet seen that done here; they're trimmed more to promote low-hanging fruit.

"In matters of principle, stand like a rock; in matters of taste, swim with the current."

Yesterday's comments about half-days are matters of taste. Plus today was a short day.

At any rate, Batou and I walked the full distance together. I did notice when we stopped for coffee in one village, a taxi immediately pulled up and then left empty when we did. It's possible the internet might not be secure.

We are spending the night in O Cebreiro, which has a church dating to the nineth century; the village is pre-Roman; population, fifty; altitude 5000 feet—it's pretty cloudy/misty up here. Every roof is thatched with wheat straw running vertically and tied in with grape vines horizontally.

Walking through the small villages today made me remember when we first moved to where Nonna and Pops live. My great-grandparents had owned forty acres there. My grandparents bought half of that, set out to build a new house for themselves, and gave five acres to Nonna and Pops on which they moved by tractor-trailer a small house and later added on a couple of times to be the house they now live in. I was four years old when we moved there. All this to say that once the land was cleared and the houses built, the bugs were so bad that my grandparents bought guineas and then bantams to help get rid of the bugs. It wasn't long before we got rid of the guineas—they make a lot of noise and poop and have a nice dark meat. We kept the bantams a little longer. They were harder to catch.

One Easter at the co-op they were selling yellow, blue, pink, and green chicks. We bought the limit and a bag of hen scratch and raised them to be pullets. The dyed feathers grew out about as fast as getting rid of highlighted hair. Have you ever heard, "running around like a chicken with its head cut off"? I have seen that spectacle.

And those chickens tasted like chicken.

I forgot to tell you about the Purple People Eaters, and Batou says not to, so good night, sleep tight.

Love,
Ba

O CEBREIRO TO TRIACASTELA

Dear Garrison and Rhys,

When we went to bed last night, we were in the mountains, but you couldn't tell it because of the Mista.

If you bumped up against a bush, water would fall all over you, but it wasn't raining. If you got off the path into the grass, your feet would be drenched, but it wasn't raining. I could see Batou walking in front of me until she was about ten feet away, then she was gone. The Mista.

I ran after her, then the Mista came for me. Swirling around me. Lifting me up and over the mountains, sticking to me the way cotton candy sticks to the handle. I became the cotton candy stick. The Mista and I were one.

It was cold. It was wet. It was everywhere. The Mista.

The Mista tied me up into a ball and rolled me through the mountains. The Mista.

I rolled into a gooey ball, rolled fast, everything sticking to me as I rolled. The Mista.

I rolled into a building where I crashed like an egg, where a witch told me to wash with warm water to break the spell of the Mista.

The witch was right.

The Mista swirled and swirled off of me and continued swirling down the drain until it was gone.

The Mista is gone.

But where is Batou?

Love,
Ba

TRIACASTELA TO SARRIA

Dear Garrison and Rhys,

Today is Tuesday. We'll be home next Tuesday night. Once again, please forgive me if I repeat something. If I haven't talked about the types of accommodations, I meant to.

I'll start with the least expensive.

While I've seen evidence suggesting people sleeping on the trail, certainly there have been no tents. And there's no reason for what we'd think of as camping. The essence of El Camino is to get back on the trail the next day and complete the pilgrimage to Santiago de Compostela, not to linger and relax. We've met one waitress who had taken a job just long enough to get herself back on the trail, but that seems to be the exception.

Next are albergues/hostels administered by the churches; then albergues/hostels administered by municipalities—both with dormi-

tory-style sleeping. Then more commercial albergues/hostels. Then small bed and breakfast establishments—usually old estates converted into private rooms and baths but shared common areas and dining. Then hotels. Last night we stayed in an interesting combination, part albergue with very inexpensive dorm rooms and part private rooms and private baths. We were lucky to have landed the latter, but having laundry facilities and other shared amenities was nice.

Long walk along the Oribio River today with thoughts of crumbling rock walls and what difference 500 years makes.

We visited one of the oldest monasteries in Spain, the Samos Benedictine Monastery, which provides albergue services and retreats to pilgrims/lay people.

There's a book titled *The Ugly American*. It was about the CIA. One of its themes was that, to effectively influence a country, you can't be ignorant of their language, culture, customs, etc, and expect their cooperation.

We've noticed some things that bear mentioning, mostly having to do with asking for help in a foreign country.

The first one that everyone has seen in a comedy is the American tourist who screams English, thinking the volume will assist in being understood. In Europe especially, they either speak a little English or they don't, and most do. The point is, they are more likely to try to help you when you at least try to speak their language.

Imagine someone coming up to us in America and expecting us to respond to them in Italian, or Greek, or whatever. That conversation probably would go nowhere, but if they approached you with, "Good morning. Please, I need some help," I bet you'd try your best to understand their needs and help them.

Batou has noticed that Spaniards are even more polite than the French and American Southerners in expecting a little banter before directly approaching an issue. The first thing said to someone each day should be, "Buenas dias; Bon jour; Good morning." Then you can ask your question in their language as best you can, even with a little English thrown in, followed by, "Por favor, s'il vous plaît, please."

Know the basics in any country you travel to; use them even at home:

> Good morning.
> Good afternoon.
> Good evening.
> How are you?
> Good-bye.
> Please.
> Thank you.
> You're welcome.
> Donkey banjo?
> Buen camino.

I've thrown around a lot more English than Spanish on this trip. At any rate, I get along very well by starting with the basics in Spanish then proceeding from there with the kindness of strangers, or Google.

Points I'm trying to make: sign up for some foreign languages while you're very young, and practice the politeness protocol in English so that it's a natural progression for you when you move into the foreign languages.

Finally, the convergence. Sarria is where a lot of pilgrims begin their journey. Gotta walk at least 100 kilometers to get the certificate of completion.

Off to octopus dinner.

Love,
Ba

SARRIA TO PORTOMARIN

Dear Rhys and Garrison,

It's hot today. In several of the villages, we noticed residents had put on their doorsteps bottles of water for pilgrims. Sometimes in a glass bottle with a note saying, "free water" or:

"Buen Camino";

usually in a recycled plastic bottle with no note, just understood.

The water for pilgrims brought back more memories from those water wells I told you about. It turned out the water was not good for much more than flushing toilets—Kimi got hepatitis, and Ronnie developed a bad case of diaper rash from all the bleach used to try to remove the iron stains from the diapers. We would drive to Spring Lake Park where there was a clear free-flowing spring with proven potability. We'd fill whatever containers we could fit in the car and have to return when that supply ran out. Unfortunately, we continued going to Spring Lake Park for drinking water, and Nonna continued carting clothes to Vickers' laundromat even after the wells were dug. I remember using the washing machines at the laundromat and then taking the clothes home wet to hang on the clothes line. Twenty cents was a lot of money to spend drying a load of clothes.

And that brings back the memory of the first time I ever steered a vehicle. We were returning to Fulton my uncle's tractor, which we had borrowed to dig the ditch for the new water line that hooked us up to community water. I was sitting in Pop's lap as we drove on the abandoned Highway 67. The new highway was built a few feet to the west. I was not a lot older than you are now. "Okay, I'm letting go of the wheel. You're the only one steering now." The tractor started veering right; I turned the wheel to the right. We almost ran off the road. "Why'd you do that?"

"I didn't think it was going to be that easy, thought there must be a trick to it."

That was my first and last driving lesson with Pops.

Sometimes I do goofy things with good intentions, but backing a trailer makes sense to me.

When we finally got hooked up to city water and finally bought a used wringer washer and two wash tubs for fifteen dollars on a kited check, for Nonna that still meant washing, wringing, rinsing, wringing, rinsing again, wringing, and then hanging out to dry on the clothes line every piece of clothing that her family of six ever wore. I recall Nonna saying, "We just need to let those soak a while." I don't know if it was because the clothes were so dirty or because she was so tired.

By the time your mom was born, disposable diapers were readily available, but when I was a kid, we'd never heard of them.

I've been told when I was an infant Pops accidentally ran a diaper pin through my thigh while changing my diaper. We never discussed it, but I do recall his saying nothing when being chided about it by his sisters

when discussing his lack of changing diapers
for the other kids.

That's enough about the good old days.

Love you.
Ba

PORTOMARIN TO PALAS DE REI

Dear Garrison and Rhys,

Happy Independence Day. I hope you have a good time celebrating this 243rd year since our founding fathers put their lives and the lives of their families and neighbors at risk in declaring independence from England. The English were bullies; now they are our allies.

When your mom was five years old, we hiked at Camp Takoda with the Indian Princesses. I thought about that 1987 hike as the trail here began to bottleneck today.

In the 80's there were published a lot of self-help/how-to-succeed-in-business books. I recall one that had the theme, maybe even the title, *Either Lead or Get Out of the Way*.

Your mom and several friends were walking a path that abruptly required quite a jump over running water. It was either make the jump to the other side, get wet, or go back.

They all stopped, looked at the water, looked at each other, then looked back to the dads. I couldn't help saying, "Someone either needs to lead, or get out of the way."

That's all it took to get your mom to make the jump. So we all finished the hike and made it back to camp in time to see Takoda shoot the burning arrow.

By the way, you had to be five years old to join that august group that by now probably has been renamed, but I knew Meg could have made the hike, so the next year she got a special dispensation as a three-year-old princess.

The bottlenecking leads me to the point, very similar to the point I was earlier trying to make about courtesy in a host country and trying to speak their language. When you're walking or biking with someone, if in doubt go single file. If someone is trying to pass, make it easy for them; don't hog the trail; don't be oblivious; do be considerate of others.

We're staying in a magnificent old farm house tonight. Way out of town. A fireplace so big there is a hoist for the cauldron that was used in it. Hams and bacon slabs are hanging in the base of the chimney, smelling good and dry curing in July. There's even an horreo—we'd been noticing those interesting corn storage buildings, but I hadn't seen the inside of one till now. Reminds me of Arkansas with the pine trees and all, but I am wearing a light vest in this cool breeze.

Love,
Ba

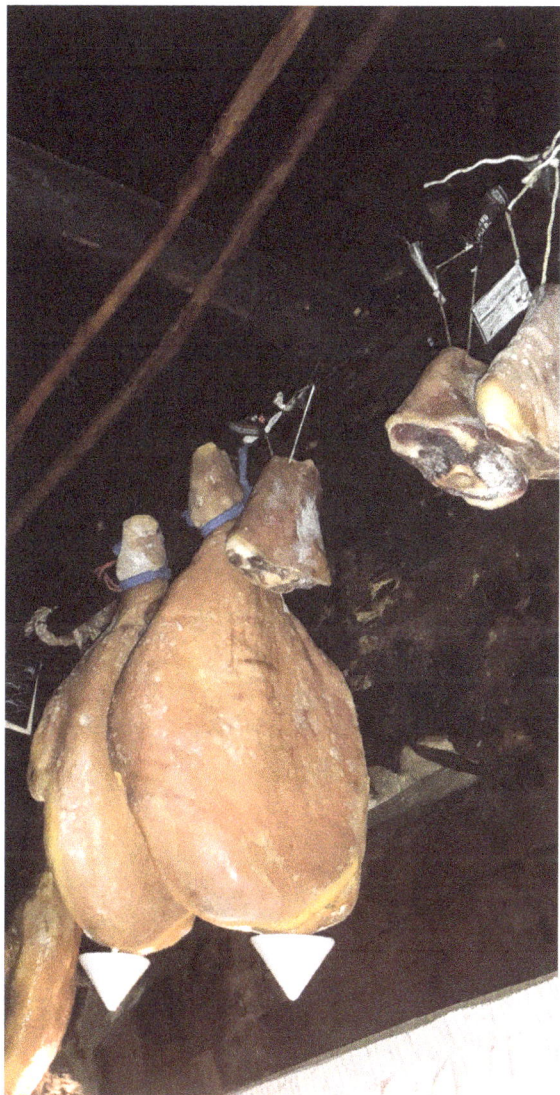

Palas de Rei to Arzua

Dear Rhys and Garrison,

Today we discovered the Fountain of Youth. That was one of the reasons the Spanish sponsored Columbus' voyages to the Americas. And here it was in northern Spain all along.

As we approached the community fountain in the town of Melide, we noticed a gentleman wearing a sweater. It was pretty warm by then. He was putting a terra cotta pitcher under the flowing water.

Batou struck up a conversation with him, learned he had been born across the street ninety-nine years ago, had lived there ever since, only drank water from that fountain, didn't drink alcohol every day, but did enjoy a little albirino with fresh wild trout, didn't eat fish otherwise because he figured they're all farmed now, grew his own vegetables, and therefore worked in his garden every day, and obviously enjoyed visiting with pretty girls.

Batou and I already had discussed doing more trout fishing, and I think Alexia already carries an albirino, so we're pretty much set. I poured the water in my canteen onto the flowers and refilled with the FOY water.

Last night at dinner our host-owners were the chief cooks and bottle washers. Actually, the man served as the waiter and taxi driver, and the woman did everything else. The place and experience were lovely, and I am not complaining about anything; I'm just setting up the observation that smart men usually marry smarter women and that this particular man, at least compared to his wife, was lazy. And that probably has nothing to do with the way he pronounced asparagus. "For the first course we have sparrows or soup." All of his guests were from English-speaking countries.

Patricia and I caught on, so she ordered the asparagus salad, and I ordered the soup. I would have gone for four and twenty sparrows had I believed it, but the lady seated across from us was astounded. "Well, I wouldn't eat that. I guess I'll have the soup."

We smiled at her and chatted a bit across the room. Long story short Josie is lovely, and she and Batou became fast friends. Indeed, they're finishing up the second half of today's Camino together as I write this.

Have you ever seen two swans necking? It's a magical sight. That's what I was reminded of today when we saw two horses staying side by side, although facing opposite directions, constantly swishing their tails. People who are around horses a lot probably wouldn't think anything about it, but I was impressed with how each kept the flies out of the other's face.

The three of us stopped for lunch today soon after the FOY. We found a nice outdoor café off a side street and were enjoying a nice lunch when a cute dog, I'll say a shih tzu, walked right beside us and the other diners and proceeded to poo on the street just a few feet away. Josie was horrified, as were the other diners who shooed it away. A few minutes later the dog sneaked back to what apparently was its favorite spot and left a huge dollop. Horrified again. Then I saw a small car bouncing too fast down the cobblestone street, tires headed right for the poo.

"Take cover." Patricia and I ducked, but I think Josie figured me for just a dry sense of humor. At any rate, I think I'd let those clothes soak a while.

Lodging tonight in a 1500-year-old house. No AC, but I've got my sweater on now.

Love,
Ba

ARZUA TO AMENAL

Dear Garrison and Rhys,

This is our penultimate night on El Camino. Tomorrow we sleep in Santiago de Compostela, the next night in London, then home. The inn we stayed at last night was a very well run machine. Before dinner, the manager approached us and said, "We serve family style, but if there is anything else you want just let us know." There was nothing else we wanted, and more.

62 degrees F at 9 A.M..

A friend who had lost an uncle who was rather young when he died once shared with me, "Yep, didn't floss; bacteria went to his heart valves, and he was gone." Did I ever tell you what makes a warning a good warning?

I sense things are about to get hectic, so this might be the last story for a while.

And if I don't tell you about the Purple People Eaters, who will?

If I don't tell you about the Purple People Eaters now, when will you know?

I couldn't believe it happened, but it did.

The birds were trying to tell us, but we were too busy with other stuff.

We were walking a beautiful trail. In retrospect, too beautiful. Everything was perfect, we thought. Too good. Too pretty. The only thing that seemed a little strange was all the chicken houses backed up to the trail.

The hedges were flowering and tall. When the hedges became trees, or when the trees began to canopy, or when tree tops bowed to the far side of the trail and took root, we didn't even stop to take pictures.

Before we knew it, we were like coons in a trap. We turned around to see the hedges running toward us. But they weren't hedges. They were Purple People Eaters, camouflaged with eucalyptus leaves all over their stinking purple bodies.

I could have impaled a few, but it only would have made things worse. They were an over-whelming army of Purple People Eaters.

Of course, if we had ever heard of them, we would have taken the alternate route, but we were captured before we knew Purple People Eaters existed.

Remember those chicken houses I mentioned? They weren't chicken houses. That's where they put us, along with scores of other pil-grims, all in an area surrounded by rock walls ten feet high with sharp fleurs de lis on top.

They took all our belongings, then wired bells around our necks.

There we were with the others clinking around the inside of the prison, thinking about how to escape. Except none of the others wanted to escape. They were afraid of the army, and they all said the food was pretty good.

The only problem was that every night the guard would choose one pilgrim to help with supper—and that pilgrim never would return.

I walked around the compound thinking. I needed a plan.

Soon the army returned with more pilgrims and then left to pillage again. As you know, Batou can size up and get to know people pretty quickly. I asked her which of the pilgrims could be trusted, and it turned out to be a lady almost as tall as I am and twice as strong. Lucky for us, because the fewer people who need to know a secret, the better; and the fewer people you need to rely on, the better.

"Would you like to escape with us?"

"No, thanks. I'm afraid of what the army would do, and the food here is pretty good. But I'll help you. Just promise me you'll tell the police in the second village from here— not the first village. The first one is where the Purple People Eaters live."

"Deal. Bargain. Quid pro quo. I will do as you ask, if you'll help us over the wall. Let's shake on it."

I looked around for materiale. There were plenty of eucalyptus leaves lying around but nothing else. I tore a roof tile from one of the chicken coops.

When the guard came for the next victim was when we were to make our move, eucalyptus leaves stuffed into the housing of the bells.

In my prime I barely could jump up and touch a ten-foot basketball rim. There was no way I could reach the top without a leg up.

Batou agreed to go first and immediately to start running for the second village, whether I made it over the wall, or not.

The army was gone. The guard came into the compound to select his next helper. Amazona was ready. Batou was ready. I was ready. As soon as the guard turned his back on us to head back to the kitchen, Batou and I silently would be over the wall.

But, as Robert Burns would say, "The best-laid plans o' Mice an' Men gang aft agley."

The guard grabbed Batou.

What to do?

"Duck."

Batou hit the ground, and I let go the roof tile.

Bullseye, pretty much. The guard went down in agony.

Seconds later, with Amazona's help, Batou was over the wall. Now it was my turn. Amazona did her part and was able to stand up with me standing on her shoulders. I could grab and hold onto the shafts of the fleurs de lis, but that was about it. I tried toe-ing up the wall, then fell back. I tried kneeing up the wall, then fell back.

The guard had recovered and was yelling. With me still holding on to the fleurs de lis, Amazona held me by the seat of my pants so that I was as close to parallel to the ground as she could get me then shotputted me to the other side.

Yes, we're both bruised, and scratched, and blistered, but we made it.

Batou is filing an official report with the authorities right now. We, at least Batou, kept our end of the bargain and are now headed home.

Love,
Ba

AMENAL TO
SANTIAGO DE COMPOSTELA

Dear Boys,

When we set out from Amenal, I told Batou, "I'm in this for the long haul." Yet, she had made it easy for me with her long walk the previous day. Today was a nice walk. No cuckoos, just love birds singing and us chickens.

For a while I have followed the Willy Nelson estate planning method—spend all your money now so as not to spoil the kids. And on this trip Batou has demonstrated she will give her last euro to the church, any church. We didn't pass a church if the doors were open, and we didn't enter a church where Batou didn't purchase a candle and light it. Everyone loves Batou, but the priests really love her. At more than one little church the priest gave her a personal tour to show her the church's history and relics. One stands

out. Inside the baptismal font, which had a cover that could slide open, the church had the biggest St. James conch shell imaginable—as big as a baby.

I learned something about Tata that I didn't know until we'd burned the last euro.

She's the same way—loves to burn candles in honor of someone she loves. At any rate, that slow moving smoke over northern Spain was us.

When we visited the monastery, we heard the obvious from the tour guide, "You've seen all those gourd shakers and rattling scallop shells the pilgrims put on their staffs and packs? A thousand years ago one had to walk all the way to Finisterre to get one of those shells from the sea to prove they had made the pilgrimage. Now landlocked Santiago de Compostela has claimed the shells as their own."

On the last day of walking, seeing pilgrims was like seeing cars on a freeway; very seldom were there times when there wasn't one in view.

DATE ET CACHET DE LA HALTE

RONCESVALLES 100 FEM AYEGUS

MONASTERIO DE SANTA MARÍA LA REAL DE IRACHE

7 Junio · 2019

IRACHE

FUENTE DEL VI... ...YEGUI · ESPAÑA

07 - 06 - 2019

Hotel Rural
orrién de Ane
...F: B71182162

08/06/2019

IGLESIA DEL SANTO SEPULCRO
TORRES DEL RIO (Navarra)

Casi... ...a   Ermita del Poyo
Lucia   ...MINO DE SANTIAGO
Te...   ...RGOTA (Navarra)

8-6-2019

HOTEL GRAN VÍA
...RISTO... HOTELERA S.A.

I didn't know what to expect upon entering the city. We had followed for quite a while a young lady obviously having a hard time walking. I don't know why I mention her except to say there was no doubt she was going to make it. Maybe she was jubilant when she stood over the 0.0 kilometer marker, but I didn't notice much jubilation from others.

The city plaza was not full. There was a lot of milling about, people taking selfies with the cathedral in the background, people just sitting on the flagstones. One couple who had walked all the way from Paris told Batou they were in awe of the cathedral and the whole experience. The sense I noticed on many was the look of, "What am I going to do now?" Indeed, some turned around and just started walking back home; some we met had decided to make their life on El Camino; others were wondering where they'd find a place to stay for the night.

I guess I expected more catharsis from others, at least, maybe even from myself.

We decided to check into the hotel and clean the dust off before Batou's standing in line to receive the official credentials or diploma, and our then seeing the inside of the cathedral together. I don't qualify for the diploma, because you have to certify that during the last 100 kilometers from Santiago de Compostela you walked the entire 100 and got at least two sellos each day in the Pilgrim Passport. Apparently they check that stuff carefully. Batou had to show further credentials to prove who she was, because after taking a shower they thought she looked too good to be a pilgrim.

We touched the tomb of apostle Saint James. Batou and I both were impressed with the marble steps leading up to and down from the relic—there was a smoothly worn wave pattern from the millions and millions of footsteps there before and with us.

We're now on the easyJet flight to London. No grape vines in my pack like the monks used to do on their goings to and comings from France. I understand the easyJet business model is to serve markets not served by other airlines. I believe that. I wouldn't want to mess with easyJet if there were any other way. I'm not complaining, merely mentioning

it to others. This has been another trip of a lifetime with the love of my life.

A thousand years ago one might make the pilgrimage as a penance at the suggestion of a priest, or perhaps, in addition to so doing, buy an indulgence into heaven.

I did notice a sign on the trail, "You have entered Paradise."

But those of you who know me know I'm in heaven right here and right now, and was almost every step of the way.

Love,
Ba

ABOUT THE AUTHOR

Gary Green, a trial lawyer in Little Rock, Arkansas, says, "If you can't tell a children's story, you can't try a case. And the answer to the existentialist is grandchildren."

www.ingramcontent.com/pod-product-compliance
Lightning Source LLC
Chambersburg PA
CBHW050822090426
42738CB00020B/3452